SIMON & SCHUSTER BOOKS FOR YOUNG READERS
An imprint of Simon & Schuster Children's Publishing Division
1230 Avenue of the Americas, New York, New York 10020
Text and photography © 2025 by Sandhya Acharya • Illustration © 2025 by Avani Dwivedi • Book design by Chloë Foglia
All rights reserved, including the right of reproduction in whole or in part in any form.
SIMON & SCHUSTER BOOKS FOR YOUNG READERS and related marks are trademarks of Simon & Schuster, LLC.
For information about special discounts for bulk purchases, please contact Simon & Schuster Special Sales
at 1-866-506-1949 or business@simonandschuster.com.
The Simon & Schuster Speakers Bureau can bring authors to your live event. For more information or to book an event,
contact the Simon & Schuster Speakers Bureau at 1-866-248-3049 or visit our website at www.simonspeakers.com.
The text for this book was set in Weidemann. • The illustrations for this book were rendered digitally.
Manufactured in China
0125 SCP • First Edition
2 4 6 8 10 9 7 5 3 1
Library of Congress Cataloging-in-Publication Data
Names: Acharya, Sandhya, author. | Dwivedi, Avani, illustrator.
Title: Living bridges : the hidden world of India's woven trees / Sandhya Acharya ; illustrated by Avani Dwivedi.
Description: First edition. | New York : Simon & Schuster Books for Young Readers, [2025] | "A Paula Wiseman book." | Includes
bibliographical references. | Audience: Ages 4–8 | Audience: Grades 2–3 | Summary: "A child learns how to care for and weave
the roots of the living tree bridges in his village in India in this narrative nonfiction story" —Provided by publisher.
Identifiers: LCCN 2024005552 (print) | LCCN 2024005553 (ebook) |
ISBN 9781665950299 (hardcover) | ISBN 9781665950305 (ebook)
Subjects: LCSH: Living root bridges—India—Juvenile literature.
Classification: LCC TG395 .A34 2025 (print) | LCC TG395 (ebook) | DDC 624.20954—dc23/eng/20240328
LC record available at https://lccn.loc.gov/2024005552
LC ebook record available at https://lccn.loc.gov/2024005553

Living Bridges
The Hidden World of India's Woven Trees

Sandhya Acharya

Illustrated by Avani Dwivedi

A Paula Wiseman Book
Simon & Schuster Books for Young Readers
New York   Amsterdam/Antwerp   London   Toronto   Sydney   New Delhi

Up in the mountains of Meghalaya, India,
under a cover of clouds,
sits my village.

When the monsoon winds blow,
the rain pours and pours
and the river overflows, spilling over its banks.

But a bridge stands tall through it all, connecting our land and people. We call it our Jingkieng Jri.

Today, Kni is going to teach me how to build our Jingkieng Jri. I can't wait!

We walk together,
hand in hand,
step in step,
down the valley,
through the mist and thicket.

I see blue earthworms squirm,
slugs slide,
and spiders scuttle by.

When we reach the clearing,
the river rumbles almost
a hundred feet below us,
and ahead,
rising, swerving, and
stretching over
a hundred feet long,
is our Jingkieng Jri.

Our Jingkieng Jri is not made of concrete or steel. It's made of roots from the tall, wide ficus trees growing on either side.

"Inside the roots live little insects, birds, and worms," Kni says. "This is their home. Our Jingkieng Jri is alive."

I follow Kni onto the bridge.
My fingers run along the gnarled sides,
and my feet step on soft, wet moss.

Midway, I peep over the side.
It's a long, long way down!
"Kni, what if the bridge gives way? What if I slip?"

"Look!" Kni says. "Teachers, vendors, farmers, doctors, and families from our village use it all the time. Our Jingkieng Jri is strong! This bridge has weathered the worst of storms." That makes me feel better,
but I decide not to look over the sides again.

We stop at a clump of new roots.
Thinner than my fingers, they hang down like vines.

"When new roots grow, we blend them with the old," Kni explains.
"We guide them along bamboo scaffolds, where they travel and lengthen, thicken and toughen, and sprout more roots of their own. Together, they make a path that we pave with mud, bark, and stone."

"Now it's time to *do*," says Kni. He begins to

weave.

One root and then another, crisscrossing them into a tight pattern.
I follow his movements, gently tugging and pulling.
The roots bend and flow, taking the shape we give them.

"Listen," Kni says.

I close my eyes and hear the river gush, the birds chirp, and the cicadas sing.

Our Jingkieng Jri is music!

Those that built the bridge before us,
and those that will come after us.
For building this treasure takes

time.

Kni says some Jingkieng Jri are young like me,
while others reach back four hundred years or more.
That's older than my great-great-great-grandparents!

It seems our Jingkieng Jri can live on forever.

But then I notice something different—a scar.
"What happened here?" I ask.
"Some people cut the roots to steal and sell the white sap," Kni says.
"It leaks out like tears."

I suddenly see a group of visitors coming our way.
One tosses a plastic bottle into a growing pile.

Look, the bridge seems to say to me. I need care.

Their loud voices drown out the music made by the water, birds, and cicadas.

Listen, the bridge seems to say. I need balance.

I realize we must do more.
Our Jingkieng Jri needs love.

Love from me,
 love from Kni,
  love from visitors,
   love from us all.

When we are finished, I look at the patterns I wove
and think of all the ones I will still make.

One day, when I am older,
I will show other children
how to look, listen, and do.
How to build our Jingkieng Jri.
Just like Kni taught me.

But there is something
that I can teach today.

As I walk farther across,
I greet others and show them the plastic
and the scars.

One by one, they join us as we clean, clear, build, and weave

together.

And when the day is done,
we invite everyone
to thank the water, wind, and trees
and to promise to keep loving
our Living Bridge,

our Jingkieng Jri.

To all who seek wonder in the world, and to all the wonder in mine
—S. A.

To the children who keep our beautiful traditions alive
—A. D.

A Note from Morningstar Khongthaw, Founder and Chairman of the Living Bridge Foundation

Living Bridges represent our War Khasi-Jaintia community. They are the centuries-old indigenous technology gifted to us over generations by our ancestors. Living Bridges are also a metaphor for the unity and coexistence of our people and nature. Living Bridges are the most sustainable applications for our future.

But I see that these bridges are declining in number and heading toward extinction. The knowledge of caring for their roots is eroding within younger generations, and the bridges are being forgotten.

That is why I started my initiative to save the bridges. My journey started in 2016 when I decided to leave everything behind and pursue my passion for saving the roots. Then in 2018 I started the Living Bridge Foundation. We grow new ficus trees, guide new roots, and build new bridges. Besides building and connecting roots in the jungle, we also try to grow new roots in the hearts of the people in our communities by sharing our knowledge. We nurture this knowledge by providing educational sessions in local institutions and workshops in many villages. We are also grateful to see that knowledge about the Living Root Bridges has spread across India and the international community through various institutions and visitors.

It is my hope that with education and awareness through the Living Bridge Foundation and its vision for the future, the living roots of love, unity, and cooperation with nature will grow in all our hearts. Together, we can become strongly connected as caretakers of the Living Bridges and the rest of our natural world.

Author's Note

The state of Meghalaya in northeastern India is mountainous, with stretches of valley, highland plateaus, and a network of rivers. With average annual rainfall as high as 470 inches (about 12,000 millimeters) in some areas, Meghalaya is the wettest place on Earth. During monsoon season, rivers often flood, cutting villages off from one another. The Indigenous people of Meghalaya built Jingkieng Jri as a way to cross the overflowing rivers. "Jingkieng Jri," Living Root Bridges, are built with rubber fig trees (*Ficus elastica*), which possess elastic properties. The local tribes and community shape the aerial roots. It takes forty to fifty years to build a bridge that lasts hundreds of years. Families often undertake a project and hand it over to the next generation and the larger community. The bridges connect villages and ensure the livelihood of the local people. It is a true example of people coming together for a solution that works for all.

Over the years, some of the bridges have faced neglect and suffered the strain of increased tourism. Conservationists are working on spreading awareness among students, locals, and tourists. Cleaning drives are regularly organized to make sure the bridges are preserved, stay strong, and continue to multiply. You can help spread awareness too. Talk to your classmates, your friends, and your family about these wonderful bridges and what impresses you most about them. Create information booths, posters, and journals that introduce more and more people to this incredible phenomenon—and consider supporting organizations like the Living Bridge Foundation.

From left to right: Sandhya Acharya (left) with Morningstar Khongthaw (right); villagers weaving the roots of Jingkieng Jri together.

Glossary and Pronunciation Guide

aerial: Midair

conservationist: Someone who studies, protects, and restores local plant and animal life

Ficus elastica: The scientific name for rubber fig trees

Jingkieng Jri (JEENG-ken juh-ree): The term for "Living Root Bridges" in Khasi (the language of one of the Indigenous communities in Meghalaya)

Kni (NEE): The word for "maternal uncle" in Khasi

Meghalaya (may-gah-luh-YAH): A state in northeastern India; means "abode of clouds" in Sanskrit

War Khasi-Jaintia (wahr kah-see jahn-tee-YAH): The name of one of the Indigenous communities in Meghalaya, India

The woven roots of Jingkieng Jri.

From left to right: A Living Bridge paved with bark, mud, and stone; a side view of the full bridge; Sandhya and a local youth crossing Jingkieng Jri.

Selected Bibliography

Allen, Timothy. "Living Root Bridges: Meghalaya, India." Timothy Allen's official website. March 21, 2011. https://humanplanet.com/timothyallen/2011/03/living-root-bridges-bbc-human-planet/.

"Jingkieng Jri: Living Root Bridge Cultural Landscapes." UNESCO World Heritage Convention. February 17, 2022. https://whc.unesco.org/en/tentativelists/6606/.

Khongthaw, Morningstar (founder and chairman, Living Bridge Foundation). Interview by the author. October 3, 2022.

Living Bridge Foundation's Facebook page. https://facebook.com/morningstarfounder/.

Ludwig, Ferdinand, et al. "Living Bridges Using Aerial Roots of *Ficus Elastica*—an Interdisciplinary Perspective." *Scientific Reports* 9 (2019). https://www.nature.com/articles/s41598-019-48652-w.

"Rangthylliang 1 Root Bridge." Wikipedia. Last edited April 2, 2023. https://en.wikipedia.org/wiki/Rangthylliang_1_root_bridge.

Rathnayake, Zinara. "The Ingenious Living Bridges of India." *BBC News*. November 17, 2021. https://www.bbc.com/future/article/20211117-how-indias-living-bridges-could-transform-architecture.

Rogers, Patrick, n.d. "Why Is Meghalaya's Botanical Architecture Disappearing?" *The Living Root Bridge Project* (blog). Accessed July 16, 2024. https://livingrootbridges.com/threats-to-meghalayas-botanical-architecture/.

Schuyler, Stephen J. "The Truth about India's Living Bridges." *Grunge*. June 16, 2022. https://www.grunge.com/897548/the-truth-about-indias-living-bridges/.

Sen Nag, Oishimaya. "Amazing 'Living Bridges' Face Threat." WorldAtlas. September 23, 2019. https://www.worldatlas.com/news/living-bridges-face-threats.html.

Various interviews with the people of Meghalaya. Conducted by the author. 2022.

Wangchuk, Rinchen Norbu. "Meet the Meghalaya Boy Working to Preserve Living Bridges That Can Last 600 Years!" The Better India. June 12, 2019. https://www.thebetterindia.com/185662/meghalaya-living-root-bridges-innovation-heritage-india/.

Yule, H. "Notes on the Kasia Hills, and People." *Journal of the Asiatic Society of Bengal* 13(2), no. 152 (1844): 612–631. https://play.google.com/books/reader?id=vBgYAAAAYAAJ&pg=GBS.PA612&hl=en.